Ready to Remote Work:

Ultimate guide to help find the remote work and maximize its benefit

Ann Adams

Ready to Remote Work:
Ultimate guide to help find the remote work and maximize its benefit

Maximize the benefits of remote work and eliminate the daily commute by leveraging the flexibility to work from a location of your choice, driving your career forward in the process. This course, led by an acclaimed expert in remote work, offers tailored strategies to enhance your remote work experience, focusing on your unique role, strengths, and objectives. With a comprehensive set of tools, the emphasis is on optimizing focus, revitalizing energy, and delivering exceptional results, moving beyond the traditional desk-bound work paradigm. Ideal for both newcomers to remote work and seasoned remote professionals, this training aims to boost productivity, foster a balanced work-life integration, and cultivate strong professional relationships despite physical distances. Discover effective strategies for a seamless remote work experience, ensuring a successful blend of personal and professional life while building meaningful connections with colleagues and clients from afar.

Learning objectives
- Illustrate the setup of an effective remote work environment.

- Outline strategies for daily and long-term management of remote work.
- Identify key questions remote workers should ask to foster relationships and trust among peers.
- Define the concept of self-care.
- Distinguish among the three distinct categories of remote work.

Table of Contents

INTRODUCTION 8

Chapter 1: How Remote Work Provides Companies a Competitive Advantage 10

    The Three Issues Remote Work Can Help With 12

    Recruitment and Retention 14

    Larger Hiring Pool 15

    Organizational Resiliency 16

Chapter 2: Getting organized for remote work 18

    Optimizing Your Tech Setup for Remote Work 21

    Enhancing Remote Work Technology 22

    Leveraging Alternative Workspaces 24

    Selecting Ideal Third Places for Remote Work 25

    Integrating Third Places into Your Remote Work Strategy 26

Chapter 3: Managing your time for remote work 28

    Incorporating Personal Tasks into Your Strategic Plan 29

    Prioritize Tasks Based on Importance and Alignment with Goals 30

    Optimizing Weekly Remote Work Management 31

    Strategizing Deadline Management in Remote Work 32

    Integrating Small Tasks and Strategic Planning in Your Remote Workweek 33

    Optimizing Your Remote Workday Structure 34

Chapter 4: Working as a remote or Hybrid team 37

    Managing your day working remotely 39

    Thriving with a Distributed or Blended Team 41

    Connecting with remote colleagues 44

Chapter 5: Overcoming Burnout: Wellness Strategies for Remote and Hybrid Employees. 47

Looking After Your Mental Health in Remote Work Settings..50

Protecting personal time while working remotely..........52

Optimizing Personal Productivity and Time Management in Remote Work 54

Chapter 6: Succeeding in Remote and Hybrid Work Environments. 57

Impressing Your Manager in a Remote Work Setting. .59

Advancing your career as a remote or hybrid worker...62

Building a Strong Remote Culture...................................65

Mastering Digital Communication and Collaboration ..67

Chapter 7: Navigating Technological Advancements in Remote Work 69

Keeping Pace with Emerging Technologies 70

Integrating New Tools and Platforms..............................73

Enhancing Collaboration with Technology.....................75

Automating Routine Tasks 78

Future-Proofing Your Remote Work Setup....................80

Chapter 8: Fostering Innovation and Creativity in Remote Work 83

Creating an Innovative Remote Work Culture 85

Idea Generation and Collaborative Creativity 87

Design Thinking in Remote Work....................................89

Leveraging Cross-Industry Insights 92

Measuring and Encouraging Innovation.........................94

Conclusion...98

INTRODUCTION

Embark on a transformative journey into the world of remote work with Ann Adams, your guide to mastering the art of working from anywhere. "Ready to Remote Work" is not just a book; it's a comprehensive course designed to redefine your work life, offering the flexibility to choose your workspace, be it a serene beach, a bustling café, or the comfort of your home office.

How can you transform remote work into an engine of success? The secret lies in finding your unique approach to working remotely. There's no one-size-fits-all method; it's about discovering what works best for you. Hi, I'm Ann Adams, a speaker and a trainer specializing in the Digital Workplace. With over 20 years of experience helping individuals and organizations thrive online, and having spent a significant portion of that time working remotely myself, I'm here to guide you through this journey.

Whether you're venturing into remote work for the first time or seeking to enhance your existing remote work setup, this book is your ally. You'll gain a wealth of practical tips and tactics that not only boost your productivity but also help you overcome common challenges, such as burnout.

This guide will take you through the nuances of setting up an effective workspace, mastering time management in a flexible work environment, and building strong connections with your team from a distance. By tackling myths and revealing the real benefits of remote work, this book empowers you to unlock greater well-being and work-life balance.

Dive into "Ready to Remote Work" to learn how to harness the freedom and opportunities that remote work provides, transforming your daily grind into an engaging, flexible, and fulfilling experience. With Ann Adams as your mentor, you're set to redefine success, making work an integral, enjoyable part of your life.

Welcome to a new paradigm of work, where you're in control, crafting a productive and rewarding remote work experience tailored just for you. Let's embark on this exciting journey together.

Chapter 1: How Remote Work Provides Companies a Competitive Advantage

Remote work, encompassing various terms like telecommuting and work from home, involves employees working outside the traditional office setting. Emerging in the 1970s with technological advancements, it gained momentum in recent decades due to internet-based tools. The COVID-19 pandemic significantly accelerated the adoption of remote work for white-collar workers globally. Advocates highlight its benefits, including cost savings, increased employee autonomy and satisfaction, environmental advantages, and wider talent pools. However, concerns exist regarding the limitations of technology in replicating in-person interactions, potential distractions, work-life balance challenges, and social isolation.

While working remotely is an excellent deal for developers and other IT professionals, you should never, ever try to sell the idea of it by touting how beneficial it is to you. That's a recipe for disaster, and it almost never works.

I worked with a guy once who tried to convince management to let him work from home because it would reduce his child care costs and commute time. Not only did he fail to sell management on the idea, but he also irritated them to the point that they never allowed him to work from home.

When I suggested that the same company should allow me to work from home so that I could be more productive without distractions, I was allowed to do so the next day.

It is very difficult to sell an idea to others based on how it will help you, but it is much easier to do so when you talk about how it will help them.

If you want to convince management that working remotely is a good idea, you need to understand what it can do for a company on a day-to-day practical level as well as at a strategic level. Allowing employees to work remotely offers tremendous value and flexibility for companies.

In other words, if you can demonstrate that it helps the other party, they are more likely to work with you. The characteristics of a remote-first (or even remote-only) workspace can really correct a lot of issues in a workplace.

These issues are roughly subdivided into three categories of problems. In this second chapter, we'll discuss these problems and how they can be mitigated using remote work. Try to consider whether your own company could benefit from remote work based on the impact of these issues.

Of course, some things might not apply to your current work environment. You must determine which are relevant and which are not so you can address those concerns with management when trying to convince them to let you work remotely.

The Three Issues Remote Work Can Help With

The first category of problems that remote work can help solve is the issue of obtaining and keeping more skilled employees.

If you ask a hiring manager at most companies these days, it's becoming harder to recruit new employees and to keep existing ones. Furthermore, because of the relative scarcity of certain types of IT professionals (software developers and security professionals especially), companies are simply forced to pay more for the same talent.

When your only leverage on the market is price, the only way to beat the competition is a bidding war. That's expensive, and it's a race toward drastically overpaying for help.

The second category of problems that remote work helps with is the category of organizational flexibility and resilience. While having a single location helps with the type of "collaboration" we lovingly outlined previously, it does introduce some downsides.

For one, requiring everybody to be in the office means that work doesn't happen when people can't get there. Traffic, inclement weather, and personal issues can mean that a company can't effectively respond to problems when people aren't in the office. Depending on where the company is located, this represents a profound risk to business continuity.

Finally, remote work can also significantly help with costs. Office space is not cheap. Not only do companies have to rent the space they use, but their employees also must live close enough for a daily commute.

The latter means that the employees also must be paid enough to live near expensive office space. This is a hidden cost that is often ignored.

Let's now take a closer look at each of these issues.

As we saw previously, some of them might be relevant to your own situation, while others aren't. Identifying them and focusing your efforts on what is relevant will greatly enhance your chances to come to an agreement with management, and to do so in a way that benefits the company.

In effect, you need to figure out which issues give you the most leverage in the discussion and go from there.

Recruitment and Retention

It's very expensive to lose employees. While exact figures are hard to come by, replacing a software developer or other IT professional can easily cost well into the five-figure range—just counting the money and time required to find, interview, and onboard a new developer.

When you consider the opportunity cost of turnover, it's even worse. It's also quite common for IT professionals to change jobs on a frequent basis, so anything that reduces the frequency of such changes constitutes a significant business advantage.

According to the 2017 State of Remote Work report, companies that allow remote work experience 25% less turnover.

Remote work is more than simply another way to get things done—it's also an effective recruitment and retention tool that allows employers to compete on more than salary and benefits.

The same report indicates that fully remote companies (companies with no corporate headquarters) were able to fill positions 33% faster than other companies.

Additionally, the 2017 report showed that managers see equal performance between their remote and on-site employees. While "merely" equal performance doesn't sound particularly compelling, bear in mind that the on-site employees are often sitting in expensive real estate that costs the company money on an ongoing basis.

It's costing more money for the same work.

In many cases, remote employees represent a significant cost savings for the same amount of work. This savings often means you can hire more people.

While discussions of employee retention often center around employees voluntarily leaving a job for a better one, that's not always the case. Sometimes employees must leave due to their own medical issues or those of their close family. In these cases, the opportunity to work remotely may mean that they can keep their current job rather than having to quit due to circumstances beyond their control.

Larger Hiring Pool

In addition to the greater ease of recruiting and retaining employees, remote work also greatly increases the size of the labor pool available at a given price to the companies that allow it.

For instance, consider the typical software company in many major cities. They'll usually have an office headquarters in a reasonably expensive area (so that the employees don't get mugged at night while leaving the office).

Any employees they manage to hire must live close enough to be able to commute to the office, and their pay must be high enough to afford doing so. While there are clearly a lot of people who will meet these criteria in almost any major city, the number of people who could afford to take a similar salary to work remotely is considerably higher.

Because employee recruitment and retention are such an expensive and time-consuming part of running a business, anything that either lowers the costs of hiring or increases the number of potential employees constitutes a significant business advantage. This is especially helpful in areas where salaries are high, the local population is not particularly tech-savvy, or where terrible commutes and gridlock make travel difficult.

Organizational Resiliency

Most inhabited parts of this planet have at least some extreme weather, geological, or social events that can disrupt work. While one can anticipate many of these issues (hurricanes, for instance), many other issues tend to give little or no warning of their impending interference in your business.

Tornadoes, earthquakes, forest fires, heavy rain and snow, and even social unrest can often seem to come out of nowhere. If they happen during a workday, these events can often mean that people are unable to reach the office, must leave early, or even get stuck in transit.

For example, I currently live in Nashville, Tennessee. While we haven't had any significant earthquakes in living memory and are insulated from coastal hurricanes, we are extremely unprepared for the sort of winter weather that happens farther north.

Chapter 2: Getting organized for remote work

Regardless of whether your workspace is a small section of your dining table or a fully equipped home office, it's crucial that this space fosters a sense of joy and concentration for you. Begin by introspecting on what environments boost your focus and overall well-being, drawing from both your in-office and remote work experiences. Consider if you prefer absolute silence and isolation for maximum productivity, or if a lively atmosphere with ambient sounds or the presence of others enhances your performance. Identify the elements that uplift your mood and energy levels throughout the day; this could be anything from abundant natural light to visually pleasing decor. While some individuals might find clutter distracting, others may find it negligible. Ensure your workspace is equipped with items that contribute to your comfort throughout your workday. For instance, I like to have a knitting project nearby to stay engaged during lengthy calls, and a collection of red lipsticks is essential for my video conference appearances. Reflect on whether staying in one spot all day suits you best, or if changing locations, such as moving to a café or another room, invigorates your work routine.

Consider the variety of tasks you undertake in your remote work setting, each requiring distinct resources and environments. For interactive tasks like video conferences or phone calls, a private, well-lit area is essential to maintain professionalism and privacy. If seclusion isn't possible, consider using noise-canceling headphones to minimize background distractions and position yourself to keep interferences out of view. Ergonomic considerations are also key: ensure your chair supports proper posture and your workspace is arranged to prevent strain during computer use. Lighting plays a significant role too; employ curtains or blinds to manage excessive natural light or introduce a ring light for enhanced visibility in dim settings. For those whose workspaces serve multiple purposes, a foldable desk could be a practical solution, allowing you to transition the area according to your needs seamlessly.

Opting for a foldable workspace can significantly streamline your daily routine, eliminating the need to clear your desk each evening. This flexibility allows for mobility within your home, enabling you to select work environments based on the nature of your tasks. For instance, I have designated a compact office space within our home for calls and meetings, a space so small that our monitor is wall-mounted. My husband has converted a closet into his office, prioritizing a functional workspace over additional storage. When engaged in creative tasks like writing, I prefer working outdoors or at a café, finding that a change of environment sparks my creativity. For less demanding activities, such as invoicing, I opt for the casual setting of our living room sofa, often with the company of my teenager and the background hum of a television show.

I encourage you to conduct an experiment: assess your tasks based on their demand for concentration and select three different locations in or around your home that you haven't used as workspaces before. Over the next week, allocate each task to one of these new spots according to the level of focus or ambient noise that suits it best. Observe how this variation in your work environment influences your productivity and overall energy throughout the day.

Optimizing Your Tech Setup for Remote Work

In remote work, your computer is the lifeline to your professional world, connecting you with tasks, colleagues, and clients. To enhance this experience, personalize your digital tools and settings to infuse a sense of pleasure and efficiency into your work routine. For instance, choose a desktop wallpaper that uplifts your mood or set a motivational phrase as your password to brighten your day each time you log in.

While your organization's IT department may specify certain applications for task management, communication, or document creation, you have the autonomy to customize your setup within those parameters. Tailor your digital environment with software that aligns with your work habits and preferences to streamline your productivity.

Consider adopting specialized apps like OneNote or Evernote for note-taking to keep your information organized and accessible. Explore tools like Coda, Airtable, or Notion, which offer customizable platforms for project management and organization, catering to users without extensive technical expertise.

Diversify your email management by exploring alternative email clients beyond the default options or web browsers. Numerous email applications are compatible with services like Outlook or Gmail, each offering unique interfaces and features to enhance your email management, helping you maintain focus and organization in your digital communications.

Enhancing Remote Work Technology

In the context of remote work, your computer serves as a pivotal link to your professional responsibilities, connecting you with colleagues and tasks. Personalizing your technological tools and configurations can significantly enhance your daily work experience. Consider setting an inspiring desktop background or adopting an uplifting passphrase for logins, adding a touch of positivity each time you access your computer.

IT departments often prescribe specific software for communications and task management, but there's room for personalization to improve efficiency and satisfaction. Adapting your tech environment to suit your preferences can streamline your workflow and boost productivity.

Incorporate specialized applications such as OneNote or Evernote for more organized and efficient note-taking. Explore platforms like Coda, Airtable, or Notion, which allow for the customization of project management tools to fit your work style, even if you're not technically inclined.

Expand your email client repertoire beyond conventional or browser-integrated options by exploring a variety of email applications that are compatible with platforms like Outlook or Gmail. Each of these applications offers unique features and user interfaces, which can significantly streamline your email management processes, leading to a more organized and efficient workday.

Utilize email filters to efficiently categorize incoming messages, enhancing your productivity. For instance, I have designated a folder specifically for newsletters. Emails containing the term "unsubscribe" are automatically directed there, under the assumption that they are newsletters. This system allows me to review such emails at my convenience. Additionally, I categorize emails where I am cc'd or bcc'd as lower priority, since they are typically for my information only. By implementing these mail rules and creating specialized inboxes, I ensure that my primary inbox is reserved for critical communications, thus optimizing my focus and time management.

Optimizing your digital tools is key to enhancing your work efficiency. Consider adopting a digital notebook like OneNote or Evernote for a more streamlined note-taking process. Alternatively, you could set up your inaugural email rule or explore templates from platforms like Coda or Notion to customize your task management system. These small adjustments can significantly improve your digital workspace's functionality.

Leveraging Alternative Workspaces

The concept of 'third places'—spaces neither at home nor the traditional office—offers a refreshing change for those accustomed to remote work. These alternative environments provide a respite from the potential monotony and distractions of a home office, shared with family, roommates, or pets, and offer a solution to the challenges of in-person meetings when your home setting isn't suitable.

Consider establishing a rotation of diverse third places to enrich your work experience. Firstly, identify tranquil locations where focus is paramount, like libraries or specific co-working spaces, ensuring productivity without the disruption of nearby conversations. Secondly, for locations conducive to meetings, explore vibrant settings such as coffee shops or restaurants, or reserve meeting rooms in co-working spaces for larger gatherings. Lastly, find spots that foster co-working and social interaction, beneficial for collaboration and a change of pace.

Integrating third places into your remote work strategy not only diversifies your work environment but also maintains your productivity and work-life balance, offering the benefits of both isolation and community as needed.

Selecting Ideal Third Places for Remote Work

Choosing a regular coffee shop as your third place can offer a sense of community, allowing you to connect with fellow remote workers and mitigate feelings of isolation. An optimal third place combines several essential elements to enhance your work experience. Comfortable, yet not overly relaxing seating is vital to maintain focus and avoid the temptation of napping. Reliable Wi-Fi and ample power outlets are crucial for uninterrupted productivity, enabling you to work efficiently on your digital tasks.

When utilizing public Wi-Fi networks in coffee shops or coworking spaces, employing a VPN is essential to safeguard your data and maintain a secure online connection. Another important consideration is the availability of clean restroom facilities, an often overlooked yet fundamental aspect of a comfortable workspace. Additionally, access to nutritious snacks can prevent disruptive hunger pangs, ensuring you remain in the zone without the need to leave for a meal.

For those whose work necessitates frequent phone calls, selecting a location that accommodates quick, non-disruptive conversations is key. Even in lively settings, the ability to step into a quieter area or outside ensures your calls don't intrude on others' space, maintaining professional etiquette. If you're driving to your third place, consider the convenience of taking calls from your car, offering privacy, and reducing background noise. These strategic choices in selecting your third place can significantly contribute to a productive and enjoyable remote work experience.

Integrating Third Places into Your Remote Work Strategy

Incorporating third places into your daily remote work routine necessitates preparation that allows for swift and effortless transitions. The goal is to facilitate such convenience that, should you desire a change in environment post-lunch, you can easily pack up and relocate. Maintaining a 'nomad kit' is an effective strategy to ensure you have all essentials at your fingertips. This kit could include an extended-length laptop charger for flexibility in seating choices, a phone charging cable, a portable battery, noise-canceling headphones or earplugs for concentration, and a selection of snacks for energy sustenance.

Additionally, consider personal comfort items that cater to your specific needs, such as hand sanitizer, hand cream, pain relief medication, and extra clothing for warmth. Taking a moment to identify potential third-place locations can enrich your remote work experience. Explore a variety of settings like libraries, coffee shops, and coworking spaces, or even the homes of colleagues open to co-working. Choose a few of these locales to test out over the coming week, possibly in the company of a colleague, to find the best fit for your work style and preferences.

Chapter 3: Managing your time for remote work

The autonomy associated with remote work offers you the opportunity to craft your own schedule, a flexibility that is maximized when paired with a comprehensive, structured approach to time management. Start by envisioning the broader objectives you wish to accomplish, setting a clear direction for the year or the upcoming quarter. Ideally, focus on no more than three primary goals that transcend routine tasks, such as acquiring a new competency, advancing in your career, or achieving a work-life balance that enhances your overall well-being.

Materialize these goals by documenting them, placing them where they remain in constant view, and consider phrasing them as if they have already been realized, which can serve as a powerful motivator. For example, affirmations like "I am a successful team manager" or "I consistently enjoy eight hours of sleep nightly" can reinforce your commitment to these objectives.

Proceed to enumerate all your responsibilities, capturing the full spectrum of your professional duties, from major, year-long initiatives to the immediate tasks of the current week or month. This list should encompass all work-related activities, regardless of whether they fall within your official role. Such an organized approach not only provides clarity but also enables you to align your daily actions with your broader, long-term ambitions, ensuring a cohesive and fulfilling remote work experience.

Incorporating Personal Tasks into Your Strategic Plan

When curating your comprehensive task list, include personal development items, such as organizing your workspace or pursuing an online course to enhance your speaking skills. Integrate these tasks into an organized table or spreadsheet, augmenting it with columns for urgency, theme, importance, and goals to facilitate a structured evaluation.

Label tasks that require immediate attention within the month as 'urgent'. Categorize each task or project under a thematic label, streamlining them into broader categories like client relations, technology, professional growth, or team dynamics. The importance column should rank the significance of each task, with '1' indicating high priority and '5' suggesting lower value.

It's common to encounter tasks that are urgent but not critically important; categorizing them accordingly helps prioritize effectively. The goals column is dedicated to aligning tasks with your primary objectives established earlier. Assign a keyword to each major goal, such as 'promotion', and tag relevant tasks that contribute to achieving these milestones.

This systematic approach not only clarifies your priorities but also empowers you to assess and adjust your focus, ensuring alignment with your overarching professional aspirations and personal development goals.

Prioritize Tasks Based on Importance and Alignment with Goals

Elevate tasks rated as 'one' or 'two' in the importance column, along with those directly contributing to your goals, to the forefront of your document. Assess the remaining tasks, particularly those marked urgent but less important, and evaluate which ones can be eliminated or deprioritized.

Since reprioritizing tasks often requires collaborative decision-making, arrange a discussion with your manager to go over your prioritized tasks and those you consider less critical. If you plan to share your list, ensure it's tailored for sharing, containing only the information you're comfortable disclosing.

In your meeting, focus on the key projects and tasks, particularly those that demand more resources or time than currently available. Explore the possibility of reallocating or removing less critical tasks with your manager's input. This is also an opportune moment to discuss overarching professional goals, like leadership development or skill enhancement, especially if they align with mutual objectives within your organization.

Optimizing Weekly Remote Work Management

Effective remote work requires vigilant time management, making it essential to start and conclude each week by evaluating your tasks and objectives. This routine is an opportune moment to align your weekly efforts with overarching goals. While numerous resources propose various methods for organizing tasks, the most effective system is the one you consistently use. If your current method effectively prevents missed deadlines and forgotten tasks, continue with it. However, if your to-do list becomes a source of stress or inefficiency, it's time to adopt a new strategy that supports your productivity and allows for personal time.

Incorporate a mechanism within your weekly planning to highlight significant projects and impending deadlines. This could be as straightforward as maintaining a visible list of key projects or having a dedicated digital document readily accessible. This approach ensures you remain focused on critical tasks while navigating your remote work week efficiently.

Strategizing Deadline Management in Remote Work

Consider establishing a dedicated deadlines calendar within your digital calendar tool, distinct from your regular work and personal calendars. Populate this specialized calendar with all your crucial deadlines, utilizing a vibrant color to ensure they stand out, and set up alerts to receive timely notifications before each due date. This method is particularly effective if traditional task management apps feel overwhelming or cumbersome.

If a consolidated task management system isn't conducive to your workflow, explore alternative approaches like maintaining a digital notebook for significant tasks or using a spreadsheet for tracking specific deadlines, such as article or report submissions. Ensure your weekly plan also allocates time for activities that support your physical and mental well-being, such as exercise or social engagements, which are vital for maintaining balance in remote work.

For handling smaller, routine tasks, consider leveraging a separate reminders application. Various platforms, including Google Calendar, Microsoft Outlook, and iOS Reminders, offer functionality to set up and manage reminders.

Even home assistants like Amazon Echo can assist in tracking these minor yet essential tasks. For example, setting a recurring reminder to submit a weekly report every Friday at 4:00 p.m. ensures consistent completion of such tasks without cluttering your main task list. This segmented approach to task management can enhance your organizational efficiency and reduce stress in your remote work routine.

Integrating Small Tasks and Strategic Planning in Your Remote Workweek

For minor tasks, pinpoint potential gaps in your schedule to address them and set specific-time reminders. This allows for flexibility, as reminders can be postponed if the timing isn't ideal. This approach can be seamlessly integrated with your strategy for utilizing third places. For example, if you plan to work from a coffee shop, consider aligning a small errand like grocery shopping if the shop is nearby, setting a reminder that aligns with your location and task.

Incorporate this method into your weekly planning, scheduling both significant tasks and smaller reminders while also reviewing your meeting commitments. A valuable tip from Bob Pozen, my co-author for "Remote Inc.," is to define your objective for each meeting you attend. Record your goals privately, ensuring they are not visible to all participants. If the purpose of a meeting is unclear, reach out to the organizer for clarification, which might reveal whether your attendance is necessary or prompt the provision of a focused agenda. This habit ensures your time is spent productively, aligning all activities, big or small, with your broader work objectives and maximizing efficiency in your remote work routine.

Optimizing Your Remote Workday Structure

The configuration of your remote workday largely hinges on the nature of your job and the tasks at hand. If your role involves constant communication, aligning your schedule with your contacts' working hours is essential. However, if you have the opportunity for solitary work, there's flexibility to tailor your day to suit your personal productivity peaks.

Reflect on your natural tendencies outside of work—consider the times when you feel most alert and energized. Utilizing these insights, you could potentially restructure your workday to harness these peak periods, which is particularly beneficial if you're coordinating across time zones. For instance, I transitioned to becoming an early riser, starting my day with email correspondence to align with clients in earlier time zones. This early start allows for a leisurely morning routine, setting a positive tone for the rest of my day.

Engage in discussions with your manager and team about designated availability hours for synchronous communications like calls, meetings, or instant messaging. Establishing clear expectations around these hours can enhance team collaboration and individual productivity, ensuring you're accessible when needed while capitalizing on your most productive periods.

Explore the feasibility of establishing periods during which you are not obliged to be available, allowing you to adjust your work hours to better suit your personal effectiveness and lifestyle needs. For instance, consider rearranging your schedule to accommodate a midday fitness class, compensating with an extra hour of work in the evening, or working on weekends to free up time for midweek volunteer commitments. Such flexibility enables you to prioritize tasks based on productivity rather than adhering strictly to conventional office hours.

A productive routine is to identify three key tasks each day that you aim to accomplish, recording them to maintain focus. Sharing these objectives with a colleague or friend can bolster accountability and motivate you to complete these essential items amidst other daily responsibilities. This strategy ensures that, regardless of additional tasks or meetings, you consistently progress on your primary goals.

By centering your workday around outcomes rather than time, you optimize your performance, aligning your efforts with when you're most effective. Discuss this approach with your manager, emphasizing that the goal is to enhance productivity, not reduce working hours. Demonstrating that this method is about maximizing your potential can align your interests with those of your employer, fostering a supportive environment for this tailored work approach.

Chapter 4: Working as a remote or Hybrid team

The configuration of your remote workday is significantly influenced by the nature of your job and the tasks at hand. If your role requires constant communication, aligning your schedule with the working hours of your contacts is crucial. However, should your work include solitary tasks, there's room to adjust your day to align with your personal productivity peaks.

Reflect on your natural routine during weekends or vacations to identify when you're most alert and inspired. These insights can guide you to rearrange your workday, capitalizing on your most productive times, which is particularly beneficial if you're coordinating with colleagues in different time zones. For example, transitioning to an early riser allowed me to synchronize with clients ahead in time, dedicating the early morning to urgent tasks followed by a relaxed personal routine, setting a positive tone for the day.

It's important to communicate with your manager and team about your availability, ensuring there's a clear understanding of when everyone is accessible for real-time interactions. By aligning your work schedule with your peak productivity periods, you can achieve a more fulfilling and efficient workday, benefiting both you and your employer.

Exploring the feasibility of flexible working hours is crucial for optimizing productivity and work-life balance. The aim is to determine if there are periods when one's presence isn't mandatory, allowing for the adjustment of work hours to better suit individual preferences and commitments. This flexibility could enable employees to engage in activities like midday yoga, volunteer work, or other personal pursuits, compensating for this time by working additional hours at more convenient times, including evenings or weekends.

To effectively implement this approach, it's recommended to start each day with a clear focus on three key tasks to accomplish, documenting these objectives to maintain accountability. This practice helps in prioritizing essential tasks, regardless of any unplanned activities or meetings that may arise. By aligning work schedules with personal productivity peaks and commitments, employees can achieve a more harmonious balance between their professional responsibilities and personal interests.

It is important to communicate this proposal to supervisors, emphasizing that the goal is to enhance productivity and job satisfaction, not to diminish work hours. Highlighting the benefits of this flexible approach can demonstrate a commitment to delivering optimal performance and results.

Managing your day working remotely

The structuring of one's workday is significantly influenced by the nature of their job and the specific tasks it entails. For individuals engaged in roles that require constant phone interaction or participation in meetings, aligning with the work schedules of collaborators or clients is essential. However, for those with roles that include solitary tasks, there may be an opportunity to tailor their work schedule to better align with their personal productivity rhythms or priorities, creating a beneficial scenario for both the employee and the employer.

Consider the times when you are not working, such as weekends or vacations, to identify your natural peak productivity periods. Are there certain times when you feel most alert, intelligent, or inspired? Leveraging these insights, you could potentially rearrange your work hours, particularly if you coordinate with team members across different time zones, to optimize your effectiveness.

For example, adapting to an early start can be advantageous if you have clients or colleagues in earlier time zones. This adjustment not only allows for timely response to overnight communications but also provides a window for personal relaxation and leisure activities, setting a positive tone for the remainder of the day.

It is crucial to have a dialogue with your supervisor and colleagues to establish mutually agreed-upon times for availability, ensuring that there is a clear understanding of when everyone is expected to be reachable for calls, meetings, or prompt message responses. This collaborative approach fosters a conducive work environment that accommodates individual preferences while maintaining team cohesion and productivity.

Explore the feasibility of identifying periods during which you are not required to be available, allowing for the reallocation of work hours to better suit your personal preferences and lifestyle. For instance, you might consider working additional hours in the evening if it enables you to take a midday break for yoga, or perhaps working a half-day on Wednesdays could facilitate volunteering, with the time made up over the weekend. Such flexibility enables you to structure your work based on priorities and tasks rather than adhering strictly to conventional work hours.

A recommended practice is to begin each day by identifying and noting down three key tasks you aim to accomplish. Sharing these objectives with a colleague or friend can foster accountability and focus. Regardless of unforeseen tasks or meetings, maintaining a focus on these priorities ensures that essential goals are met.

By organizing your workday around tasks rather than time, you align your schedule with periods of peak productivity and personal well-being. Discuss this approach with your supervisor, emphasizing that the goal is to enhance efficiency and output, not to reduce working hours. This strategy demonstrates a commitment to maximizing your professional effectiveness and aligning it with personal well-being.

Thriving with a Distributed or Blended Team

In a traditional office setting, observing your colleagues' interactions and team dynamics is straightforward. You can notice how individuals engage during breaks or their behavior post-meetings, and whether they prefer informal chats or formal discussions for addressing queries with their superiors. However, these observational cues are absent in remote work environments, making it challenging to discern effective collaboration methods, particularly when integrating with a new team or initiating a fresh project with unfamiliar teammates.

Establishing clear communication norms is essential when forming or joining a remote team or commencing a new collaborative endeavor. To navigate these challenges, it's beneficial to address three pivotal questions early in the collaboration process, although it's never too late to seek clarity. Firstly, inquire about preferred communication methods. Different individuals have varying responsiveness to emails or phone calls, so understanding the preferred communication channels of your boss, clients, or teammates is crucial. For instance, a remote client might not respond promptly to emails due to high volume, suggesting alternative methods like texting for urgent matters. By clarifying these preferences, you can enhance efficiency and foster better collaboration within your remote or hybrid team.

Once I adapted to my client's preferred communication style by texting for quick decisions, our workflow improved significantly, making her one of my most responsive clients. This experience underscores the importance of directly asking your team members or clients about their preferred communication methods and the level of detail they expect in updates. Whether they prefer real-time updates or periodic summaries can only be determined through inquiry.

Addressing the frequency and nature of meetings is another critical aspect. Reducing superfluous meetings can lead to misalignment, especially with colleagues accustomed to conventional modes of communication. Establishing a consistent meeting schedule and pre-defining the use of that time can enhance synchronization. For example, organizing bi-weekly check-in sessions, with the option to cancel if pre-meeting communications resolve the agenda, can optimize efficiency and is generally welcomed by all team members. Ensuring there's a set agenda shared in advance aids in maintaining focus and productivity during these interactions.

Lastly, fostering a mutual understanding of personal backgrounds and working styles is vital, especially in remote settings where face-to-face interactions are limited. Learning about each other's personal circumstances can build trust and adaptability within the team, contributing to a more cohesive and understanding work environment.

For instance, I always inform my colleagues and clients that I work remotely while homeschooling my teenager, who is on individual school plan. Although I'm accustomed to managing work alongside my home responsibilities, there are rare occasions when I must abruptly end a call due to an emergency. By being transparent about this aspect of my life, I set a precedent for understanding, so when unexpected situations arise, even if infrequently, my team is already aware and accommodating.

This upfront disclosure fosters an environment where others feel comfortable sharing their personal constraints or challenges, enhancing mutual understanding and trust. Such openness from the beginning lays a strong foundation for our collaborative efforts, emphasizing empathy and adaptability within our professional relationships.

Connecting with remote colleagues

Establishing trust within a team enhances overall performance and collaboration. Various dimensions of trust include direct and honest communication, dependability in fulfilling commitments, respectful treatment, support among team members, and the provision of constructive feedback. Developing and maintaining these trust facets can be challenging, particularly in remote or hybrid work settings, where traditional, face-to-face relationship-building practices are not feasible.

While humanity has a long history of forging relationships in person, the digital realm requires novel approaches to cultivate trust. While informal virtual gatherings can foster camaraderie, they may not directly contribute to building trust in professional contexts, such as during crucial business presentations or client interactions. Therefore, it's essential to embed trust-building activities within everyday work engagements.

Initiating meetings by acknowledging each participant, encouraging light-hearted dialogue, balancing feedback with specific commendations, and allowing some leeway for casual discussions can contribute significantly to relationship development within the team. Additionally, being a reliable and trustworthy team member sets a standard, encouraging others to reciprocate, thereby fostering a dependable and supportive team environment.

Exemplify the behavior you wish to observe in your colleagues. Ensure that your written communications, such as emails or text messages, are professional and respectful, as if you were speaking face-to-face. Only commit to deadlines you are confident you can meet, and communicate proactively about any potential delays, providing realistic updates on your progress.

Given the reduced face-to-face interaction in remote or hybrid settings, enhance your communication efforts. If an immediate detailed response to an email isn't feasible, acknowledge the message and indicate when a reply can be expected. For those who are not in the office as frequently, consider arranging additional touchpoints with colleagues or supervisors, potentially through casual phone conversations during a walk, to maintain connection.

Be mindful of the diverse experiences and perceptions of remote work within your team. Expressing dissatisfaction about partial office attendance may not resonate well with those who are office-based full-time. Similarly, discussing feelings of isolation when others may be managing work amidst family responsibilities could create disconnects. Understanding and respecting the varied contexts in which your teammates work is crucial for nurturing a cohesive and empathetic team environment.

Complaining about the size of your home office to a colleague who manages their tasks in a shared, cramped space can undermine trust. It's vital to recognize that trust is more easily damaged than built. If a text or comment during a call bothers you, address it directly rather than via email, where misinterpretations are common. Opt for a phone conversation or a simple message requesting a chat to clarify intentions or actions, approaching the dialogue with genuine curiosity rather than assumptions.

This approach to building and maintaining relationships isn't just an additional task—it's an integral aspect of your professional responsibilities. Fostering positive interactions and understanding within your team is a crucial component of your role, essential for cultivating a supportive and effective work environment.

Chapter 5: Overcoming Burnout: Wellness Strategies for Remote and Hybrid Employees.

Establishing trust within a professional setting enhances productivity and collaboration. Various forms of trust are essential, including direct and honest communication, reliability in fulfilling commitments, respectful treatment, and providing constructive feedback for improvement. Building and maintaining these trust aspects is challenging, particularly in remote or hybrid work environments where traditional face-to-face interaction cues are absent.

We have centuries of evolved practices for building relationships in person, yet navigating online relationship-building is relatively new territory. While informal virtual engagements like online coffee breaks can foster camaraderie, they may not suffice for cultivating trust in critical work scenarios, such as during sales presentations or customer service engagements.

To develop trust within the context of work, consider initiating meetings by personally greeting each participant and promoting a brief, friendly exchange. When offering feedback via email or documents, balance critiques with specific commendations to reinforce positive behavior. Allowing some leeway for digressions during meetings can also contribute to team bonding, provided they do not significantly disrupt the agenda. Such strategies are not merely niceties but fundamental elements of building a cohesive and trusting team dynamic in a remote or hybrid setting.

Being a reliable and trustworthy individual is as vital as identifying trustworthy colleagues. Exhibit the behaviors you expect from others to establish yourself as a dependable team member. This includes maintaining transparency in communications—avoid saying anything via digital means that you wouldn't say in person. Commit only to achievable deadlines and proactively communicate any delays, providing updated timelines for your tasks.

Given the reduced physical interactions with colleagues in remote or hybrid settings, it's imperative to enhance communication. If an immediate response to an email isn't feasible, acknowledge receipt and indicate when a comprehensive reply will follow. For those less present in the office, proactively seek additional opportunities to connect with teammates or supervisors, potentially through casual calls during a walk.

Acknowledge the diverse experiences of your team members regarding remote work. Expressing dissatisfaction about partial office attendance may not resonate well with colleagues who are office-bound or facing different challenges, such as managing work with children at home. Understanding and respecting each team member's unique situation fosters a more inclusive and supportive work environment.

Voicing concerns about the constraints of your home office to someone working in a shared, cramped space may seem insensitive. Trust is fragile and more readily broken than built. If a comment in a text or during a call upset you, address it directly through a phone call rather than an email, which can lead to misunderstandings. Initiate a conversation with a simple message asking for a moment to discuss, and approach the dialogue with genuine curiosity, seeking clarification rather than making assumptions.

Building and maintaining relationships in the workplace is not an ancillary task; it is integral to your professional responsibilities. Effective communication and understanding are foundational to creating a positive and productive work environment, highlighting the importance of interpersonal interactions in achieving collective success.

Looking After Your Mental Health in Remote Work Settings.

Self-care encompasses both physical and mental well-being, necessitating strategies to maintain mental and emotional balance throughout your workday. It's crucial to establish a routine for monitoring your mental health and seeking assistance when needed. This routine should incorporate planned social interactions, recognizing the inherent need for connection, particularly for those living alone or working remotely.

When structuring your day, consider incorporating breaks that genuinely rejuvenate you, rather than activities that leave you feeling disengaged or indifferent. Evaluate your current break habits and replace ineffective routines with activities that genuinely refresh and energize you, whether it's engaging in a favorite hobby, connecting with a friend, or enjoying a solitary activity that brings you joy.

Even if you're not naturally sociable or live with others, ensuring adequate social interaction is essential, as remote work can amplify feelings of isolation, sometimes more acutely for introverts. Extroverts might naturally seek out interaction, but introverts must also be proactive in maintaining connections to counter the isolation inherent in remote work environments.

Studies indicate that introverts may find remote work challenging due to insufficient social interaction, as the daily commute to an office inherently provides opportunities for engagement. As an extrovert, I understand the effort required to arrange social activities after a day filled with virtual meetings. My solution is to establish regular co-working sessions with a friend each week, offering a refreshing change from family interactions and a chance for casual conversation during work breaks.

Establishing a systematic approach to mental health self-evaluation is essential, incorporating activities like daily meditation, mood journaling, engaging in peer support groups, or community classes. These methods are vital for integrating mental health care into daily life, ensuring it receives as much attention as work-related duties.

Leverage mental health resources provided by your employer, such as coverage or online counseling services. Regular consultations with a mental health professional can offer insights into behavioral patterns that may affect your well-being, even if you opt for less frequent sessions. My remote work experience has underscored the importance of daily self-care routines, which vary from therapy sessions and social walks to reading for leisure, contributing to overall wellness and work-from-home productivity.

Create a list of social activities and mental health practices that benefit you. Each week, select one activity from each category to incorporate into your schedule, ensuring a balanced approach to professional and personal well-being.

Protecting personal time while working remotely

Navigating the blurred boundaries between work and home life is one of the remote working model's most significant challenges and advantages. The impact of this overlap largely depends on an individual's ability to integrate work within their broader life context. It's important to emphasize that maintaining a balance isn't solely about managing work alongside caregiving responsibilities. Every individual, regardless of their family or living situation, is entitled to a fulfilling life that doesn't mandate constant availability for work-related communications.

For many years, I felt an obligation to be perpetually accessible to my colleagues and clients. This perspective shifted dramatically when I needed to adjust my work commitments to support my autistic son during his early school years. This personal experience underscored the necessity of setting boundaries to prioritize personal well-being and family, leading to a transformation in my professional approach and the type of work I engage in.

This shift also transformed my personal approach to work. I've become adept at establishing boundaries regarding my availability, enhancing my job performance by allowing me to dedicate focused attention and creativity to my tasks, free from exhaustion. However, setting these boundaries, particularly with superiors or in response to late emails, can be challenging.

To safeguard your personal time, initiate a dialogue with your supervisor and colleagues about mutually agreed-upon hours for checking and responding to emails and messages. The tendency to respond to evening emails often stems from perceived expectations, but as a team, you can establish that it's unnecessary to respond to communications between, for instance, 5:00 PM and 9:00 AM. Utilize the 'send later' function for emails composed outside of business hours, reinforcing the norm that after-hours responses are not obligatory, thereby helping to manage expectations around your availability.

When faced with an overwhelming workload, it's crucial to engage your manager in prioritizing tasks, which helps illustrate the necessity of making trade-offs. For instance, if you're tasked with completing a report and simultaneously asked to plan an event, it's beneficial to seek clarity on which assignment takes precedence to ensure quality output.

Additionally, to truly disconnect at day's end, consider turning off notifications or logging out of work devices and accounts. Setting up distinct user profiles on your computer can segregate work from personal use, enabling relaxation without the constant presence of work-related alerts. This separation helps in establishing a clear boundary between work and leisure time, crucial for relaxation and disengagement from professional responsibilities.

Adopting these strategies to delineate work from personal time can significantly enhance the remote work experience, offering more space to enjoy a well-rounded and fulfilling life. This approach has personally proven to be effective in balancing my professional and personal life, reinforcing the value of setting firm boundaries.

Given the context and content of the previous subchapters for Chapter 6, which focus on building a strong remote culture and mastering digital communication and collaboration, a fitting addition could be a subchapter centered on enhancing personal productivity and time management in a remote setting. Here's a proposed subchapter:

Optimizing Personal Productivity and Time Management in Remote Work

In remote work, where supervision is less direct, personal accountability becomes key. This section could delve into how remote workers can cultivate a sense of responsibility for their tasks and outcomes, encouraging a proactive approach to their duties.

Structuring Your Workday for Maximum Efficiency

- Task Prioritization: Provide strategies for identifying and prioritizing high-impact tasks, using methods like the Eisenhower Matrix or the Pareto Principle (80/20 rule) to differentiate between urgent and important tasks.

- Time Blocking: Introduce the concept of time blocking to allocate specific hours for focused work, meetings, and breaks, enhancing control over one's workday and minimizing the risks of multitasking and distractions.

- Setting Boundaries: Discuss the importance of setting clear boundaries between work and personal life, including establishing a dedicated workspace, defining work hours, and communicating availability to colleagues and family members.

Leveraging Technology for Productivity

- Productivity Apps: Highlight a variety of tools and apps that can aid in time management, project tracking, and focus, such as Pomodoro timers, project management software, and distraction blockers.

- Digital Minimalism: Address the benefits of digital minimalism, encouraging workers to streamline their digital tools and platforms to reduce cognitive load and enhance concentration.

Regular Review and Adjustment

- Weekly Reviews: Advocate for weekly reviews of accomplishments and setbacks to adjust plans and strategies, ensuring continuous improvement and alignment with professional goals.

- Feedback Loops: Encourage establishing regular feedback loops with supervisors or teammates to gain insights on performance and areas for growth, fostering a culture of continuous learning and adaptation.

Effective time management and personal productivity are vital in the remote work environment, where traditional office structures are absent. By adopting these strategies, remote workers can enhance their efficiency, achieve their objectives, and maintain a healthy work-life balance, contributing to their overall success and satisfaction in their roles.

Chapter 6: Succeeding in Remote and Hybrid Work Environments.

To ensure remote work is effective, enjoyable, and sustainable, it's essential to consider its integration into your broader work life. This often involves creating opportunities for interaction within your workweek, whether through client meetings, occasional office days in a hybrid setup, attending industry events, or co-working in communal spaces like coffee shops. The ideal balance between remote and in-person engagement varies based on individual preferences and the nature of your work.

Begin by evaluating the extent of your independent tasks, which are those you can carry out solo from inception to completion. Next, assess the interdependent aspects of your role, where collaboration with colleagues on different segments of a project is crucial, even though each person may have distinct responsibilities. For instance, a member of a merchandising team might focus on a specific aspect, such as packaging, that contributes to the collective outcome.

Lastly, consider collaborative tasks that necessitate real-time teamwork, like a strategy team making joint decisions or an event team managing live online events. Understanding these work dynamics can guide you in structuring a remote or hybrid work approach that aligns with both your job requirements and personal work style.

For those with a significant amount of independent work, remote working is likely preferable due to the reduced likelihood of interruptions, facilitating concentration on tasks requiring deep focus. Conversely, if your role involves considerable interdependent work, strategize by categorizing your tasks: separate those you can perform independently from those requiring synchronization with teammates. Allocate time for focused individual work at home and designate specific periods for collaboration, whether it's transitioning tasks to colleagues, receiving briefings, or preparing for your next assignment.

For roles heavily reliant on collaboration, real-time interaction with team members or clients becomes essential. For individuals in national or global teams, this often means virtual meetings. However, if your collaborators are locally based, consider aligning your schedules to enable in-office collaborations or face-to-face work sessions, enhancing the efficiency and effectiveness of your joint efforts.

Even if most of your tasks are independent or your team members are located in different cities or countries, consider spending some time in the office when possible. Engaging in face-to-face interactions with clients or colleagues can significantly enhance relationship building, collaboration, and provide a broader perspective on team and organizational dynamics. Maximize your office visits by focusing on interactive activities; aim to engage extensively with your colleagues to make the most of your in-person time.

Then, allocate your remote working days for concentrated solo work, which benefits from the quiet and controlled environment of your home office. These are the days to immerse yourself in tasks that require deep focus, potentially scheduling blocks of time or entire days without meetings to facilitate uninterrupted productivity. This strategic division of your workweek can help you harness the unique advantages of both remote and in-office work settings.

Impressing Your Manager in a Remote Work Setting.

Cultivating a strong relationship with your boss or clients requires intentional effort, particularly in a remote work environment where the "out of sight, out of mind" risk is real.

Prioritize establishing regular communication channels, such as bi-weekly one-on-one meetings if you're part of a fully remote team. Additionally, participate actively in any casual online gatherings or team-building activities organized by your boss.

For those with bosses who work on-site, align your schedule to ensure some overlap in the office. If your boss is based in a different city, explore opportunities for occasional in-office visits. Communication extends beyond meetings and calls; clarify with your boss or clients their preferred frequency and mode of updates, whether through emails, messages, or scheduled meetings.

When it comes to keeping your boss informed, it's advisable to lean towards overcommunication, especially regarding potential issues or delays. Understanding your manager's preference for problem-solving involvement is crucial—some may prefer you attempt to address challenges independently, while others are willing to assist in troubleshooting. Engage directly with your boss to seek their input and establish clear expectations for communication and problem-solving approaches.

Understanding how your boss prefers to collaborate is crucial, and utilizing their feedback can enhance your problem-solving skills. When seeking guidance via email, prioritize posing your question promptly, followed by necessary context or background information. This approach aligns with the preferences of many managers who may not have the time to sift through lengthy emails. A succinct query and an initial suggestion for action, followed by additional details as needed, can be more effective and appreciated in a busy work environment.

As someone who has been on both sides of the managerial relationship, I've learned the value of concise communication. While detailed emails have their place, clarity and brevity often lead to greater appreciation and efficiency. Additionally, regular performance reviews, ideally semi-annually, are vital for discussing broader career and performance goals, ensuring alignment with organizational objectives and personal development plans.

Establish clear benchmarks for success with your boss, identifying specific, trackable metrics such as sales numbers, website traffic, or customer satisfaction scores to gauge your progress. Regular feedback sessions, whether weekly, biweekly, or monthly, are essential for receiving performance evaluations and developmental coaching.

View any critiques as chances for growth, and proactively seek positive feedback to understand your strengths and areas for enhancement. Asking for this feedback can help you identify successful strategies to continue and expand upon.

While striving to exceed expectations, ensure that your efforts to go above and beyond do not detract from your primary responsibilities or consistently infringe upon your personal time. Volunteering for additional tasks, like assisting a team member or leading a community initiative, can significantly bolster your visibility and reputation within the organization. Demonstrating such commitment and teamwork can make you a standout employee, even in a remote setting.

Advancing your career as a remote or hybrid worker

Regardless of whether remote work is a permanent aspect of your career or a temporary or part-time situation, it's crucial to strategize how your current work can pave the way for future growth opportunities. Remote work, when approached strategically, can position you for upcoming promotions or new job opportunities by delivering outstanding results and maintaining visibility within your team and industry.

If you're in an environment where peers are frequently in the office while you work remotely, leverage this by taking on tasks that are challenging to accomplish in a busy office setting. This could include handling sensitive conversations that require privacy or engaging in intensive projects that demand uninterrupted focus. For example, I carved out a niche as a data journalist by focusing on comprehensive, data-intensive projects, which would be difficult to manage in a bustling office environment.

However, it's important not to rely solely on the quality of your work to make an impact. Ensure that you're actively engaging with your team and clients, making your presence felt and your contributions known. Whether it's through virtual platforms or occasional office visits, being proactive, helpful, and collaborative helps reinforce your reliability and value to the team.

Implementing effective email management strategies can enhance your reputation as a responsive and reliable communicator, known for prompt replies and assistance. By setting aside specific times for group messaging, you can actively contribute to team discussions, not only responding to direct queries but also participating in broader conversations where your knowledge is applicable. Aim to be the go-to team member whom others rely upon for support and information.

Maintain a performance file to document your achievements and accolades from colleagues and clients. This record should include instances of positive feedback and notable accomplishments, which can be instrumental during performance evaluations or discussions regarding career advancement.

Expanding your visibility beyond your immediate organization is also beneficial, offering potential career opportunities and enabling you to introduce fresh insights and connections to your current role. This broader engagement can contribute to your professional development and the value you bring to your team.

Engage with a professional network in your field by joining relevant groups or attending industry events, which can be in person or online. This exposure broadens your professional circle and provides opportunities for learning and collaboration. Consider establishing a presence on platforms like LinkedIn or start a blog or podcast to share your expertise and insights with others in your industry. Rather than viewing this as personal branding, approach it to contribute valuable knowledge and foster community within your field.

If you're unsure about your content, consider featuring interviews with industry peers or summarizing insightful articles, positioning yourself as a conduit for collective learning and growth. Embracing generosity in sharing knowledge not only enhances your professional development but also establishes you as a valuable and collaborative team member and industry peer. Leverage the adaptability afforded by remote work to support others in your team and broader professional community, thereby enhancing your desirability as a colleague and potential candidate for advancement.

Building a Strong Remote Culture

In the realm of remote work, the essence of a company's culture transcends physical boundaries, becoming a cornerstone for team cohesion and employee satisfaction. A strong remote culture is anchored in clear communication, shared values, and mutual trust, creating an environment where employees feel connected, valued, and motivated.

Strategies for Fostering a Sense of Belonging

- Virtual Team Building: Implement regular virtual team-building activities that are not just fun but also meaningful, encouraging team members to share personal stories, celebrate milestones, and support each other's achievements.

- Transparent Communication: Establish open channels for communication, encouraging team members to voice their ideas, feedback, and concerns. Regular town hall meetings, AMA (Ask Me Anything) sessions with leadership, and transparent decision-making processes reinforce a culture of openness.

- Shared Goals and Values: Clearly articulate the company's mission, values, and goals, ensuring that every team member understands how their work contributes to the larger picture.

This alignment fosters a sense of purpose and collective effort.

Creating Virtual Spaces for Informal Interactions

- Digital Watercoolers: Designate virtual spaces where team members can gather informally, sharing personal updates, hobbies, or interesting finds, mimicking the watercooler conversations of a traditional office.

- Interest-Based Groups: Encourage the formation of virtual clubs or groups based on shared interests or hobbies, fostering interpersonal relationships beyond work-related tasks.

Case Studies: Successful Remote Cultures

- Highlight examples of companies that have excelled in building vibrant remote cultures. Detail their approaches, such as unique virtual team-building activities, innovative communication platforms, or exceptional support for employee well-being.

- Analyze the impact of these strategies on employee engagement, retention, and productivity, providing actionable insights for readers.

Building a strong remote culture is an ongoing, dynamic process that requires intentionality and commitment from every level of the organization. By prioritizing connection, communication, and shared values, companies can cultivate a remote culture that not only attracts top talent but also nurtures their growth and satisfaction, paving the way for sustained success in the evolving landscape of work.

Mastering Digital Communication and Collaboration

In a remote setting, the nuances of communication become magnified, with every message, email, or video call playing a pivotal role in maintaining clarity and cohesion within teams. Mastering digital communication involves understanding its challenges and adopting practices that promote clarity, empathy, and effectiveness.

Guidelines for Effective Digital Etiquette

- Clarity and Conciseness: Encourage the practice of clear and concise communication. Emphasize the importance of getting to the point swiftly while ensuring the message is complete and considerate of the reader's time.

- Tone Awareness: Highlight the challenge of interpreting tone in written communication. Advocate for the use of positive language, careful choice of words, and when in doubt, leaning towards over-clarification to prevent misinterpretation.

- Responsive Communication: Stress the importance of timely responses while respecting boundaries. Establish expected response times within the team to avoid ambiguity.

Selecting and Utilizing Collaboration Tools

- Tool Assessment: Provide a framework for selecting the right digital tools based on team size, communication preferences, and specific needs. Consider aspects like integration capabilities, user-friendliness, and security.

- Best Practices: Once tools are selected, outline best practices for their use, including regular updates, training sessions, and guidelines to ensure everyone is proficient and comfortable with the chosen technologies.

Optimizing Virtual Meetings

- Agenda Setting: Emphasize the importance of having a clear agenda for every meeting, shared in advance, to ensure participants are prepared and objectives are clear.

- Engagement Techniques: Discuss methods to keep virtual meetings engaging, such as encouraging participation, using interactive elements, and maintaining a dynamic pace.

- Actionable Outcomes: Ensure that every meeting concludes with clear action items, assigning responsibilities and deadlines to facilitate accountability and follow-through.

Mastering digital communication and collaboration is a cornerstone of successful remote work. By adopting effective communication practices, choosing the right tools, and optimizing virtual interactions, remote teams can achieve high levels of productivity and collaboration, ensuring that distance becomes a mere logistical detail rather than a barrier to success.

Chapter 7: Navigating Technological Advancements in Remote Work

In the ever-evolving landscape of remote work, staying at the forefront of technological advancements is not just an option; it's a necessity. The chapter "Navigating Technological Advancements in Remote Work" is designed to be your compass in the dynamic world of digital transformation, guiding you through the maze of emerging technologies and equipping you with strategies to harness these innovations for enhanced productivity and communication.

As remote work becomes increasingly prevalent, the tools and platforms we rely on are evolving at an unprecedented pace. This chapter delves into the critical need for remote professionals to remain agile learners, adept at adopting new technologies that can streamline workflows, foster collaboration, and drive efficiency in a distributed work environment.

We will explore the importance of keeping pace with technological trends, not just to stay relevant, but to seize opportunities to elevate your remote work experience. From choosing the right tools to integrating them seamlessly into your daily routines, this chapter provides a roadmap for building a tech-savvy remote workspace that not only keeps you connected but also propels you ahead in your career.

Whether you're a solo freelancer, part of a remote team, or leading a distributed workforce, understanding and embracing technological change is key to staying competitive and productive. This chapter will empower you with the knowledge and tools to navigate the digital transformation in remote work, ensuring you're not just keeping up but leading the way in this digital era.

Keeping Pace with Emerging Technologies

In the realm of remote work, the technological landscape is akin to shifting sands—constantly evolving, bringing new tools and platforms to the forefront. To thrive in this environment, staying abreast of emerging technologies is not just beneficial; it's imperative. This subchapter explores strategies to remain informed and adaptable, ensuring that you're not only keeping up with the pace of change but also leveraging it to enhance your remote work experience.

Understanding the Landscape of Emerging Technologies

Begin by developing a broad understanding of the current technological trends influencing remote work. This knowledge isn't just about the latest gadgets or apps; it's about recognizing the shifts in digital communication, collaboration tools, and productivity platforms. Familiarize yourself with the technologies shaping the future of remote work, such as cloud computing, AI, machine learning, and virtual and augmented reality.

Strategies for Continuous Learning and Adaptation

Continuous learning is the cornerstone of staying relevant in a tech-driven remote work environment. Create a personal learning plan that includes following industry blogs, subscribing to tech-focused newsletters, and participating in relevant webinars and online courses. Embrace a mindset of lifelong learning, where the goal is not just to accumulate knowledge but to apply new insights and technologies in your work.

Leveraging Online Resources and Communities for Tech Updates

The internet is a treasure trove of resources for keeping updated on technological advancements. Engage with online communities, forums, and social media groups where professionals discuss and share the latest in tech. Platforms like LinkedIn, Reddit, and specific industry forums can be invaluable for gleaning insights from peers and experts alike.

Implementing a Personal Technology Update Plan

Develop a systematic approach to integrating new technologies into your work. This could involve setting aside regular time each week to explore new tools, trial software that could enhance your productivity, or review the latest updates to your existing tech stack. Prioritize learning and experimentation, and don't hesitate to discard tools that don't add value to your work.

The Role of Curiosity and Experimentation in Tech Proficiency

Curiosity is a powerful driver in the quest to stay technologically adept. Cultivate a curiosity-led approach to learning, where experimentation and the application of new tools are encouraged. This proactive stance on technology adoption can lead to innovative ways of working and problem-solving, setting you apart in the remote work landscape.

By embracing these strategies, you can transform the rapid pace of technological change from a challenge into a significant career advantage. Keeping pace with emerging technologies not only ensures that your remote work setup is efficient and modern but also demonstrates your commitment to professional growth and adaptability—a trait highly valued in the ever-evolving world of work.

Integrating New Tools and Platforms

With an ever-expanding array of tools and platforms designed to facilitate remote work, integrating new technologies into your workflow is pivotal for enhancing productivity and communication. This subchapter outlines a structured approach to selecting, testing, and adopting new digital tools, ensuring they align with your work requirements and add tangible value to your remote work environment.

Assessing and Choosing the Right Tools for Your Needs

The first step in integrating new tools is to assess your current workflow and identify any gaps or inefficiencies that technology could address. Evaluate tools based on their potential to enhance communication, collaboration, task management, and overall productivity. Prioritize tools that offer seamless integration with your existing tech stack, ensuring a cohesive and streamlined workflow.

Balancing Between Cutting-edge and Proven Technologies

While it's tempting to adopt the latest technology, it's crucial to strike a balance between cutting-edge tools and those with a proven track record. Assess the maturity of new technologies, considering factors like user reviews, developer support, and the tool's longevity in the market. Opt for tools that offer a stable user experience and reliable customer support, especially for critical aspects of your work.

Best Practices for Integrating New Tools into Your Workflow

Integrating a new tool requires a thoughtful approach to ensure it complements your existing processes. Start with a pilot phase, using the tool for specific tasks or projects to evaluate its effectiveness. Provide training and resources if you're introducing the tool to a team and establish clear guidelines on how and when the tool should be used to avoid confusion and overlap with existing tools.

Overcoming Challenges in Adopting New Technologies

Resistance to change is a common challenge when introducing new technologies. Address this by highlighting the benefits of the tool and involving team members in the selection process. Address any technical challenges swiftly and provide a feedback mechanism for users to share their experiences and suggest improvements.

Encouraging Team Adaptation to New Tools

For new tools to be effective, team adaptation is crucial. Encourage a culture of open communication where team members can express their opinions and experiences with the tool. Recognize and reward quick adopters and problem solvers who contribute to a smoother integration process. Regularly review the tool's impact on workflow and productivity, adjusting as needed to ensure it continues to meet the team's evolving needs.

By following these guidelines, you can ensure that the integration of new tools into your remote work environment is strategic, purposeful, and conducive to enhanced productivity and collaboration. The right tools, when effectively integrated, can transform the way you work, enabling you to stay connected, agile, and ahead in the digital work landscape.

Enhancing Collaboration with Technology

In the realm of remote work, technology serves as the bridge that connects disparate teams, enabling seamless collaboration across different time zones and locations. This subchapter delves into how remote workers can leverage technology to foster a collaborative environment that not only enhances productivity but also builds a sense of team cohesion and synergy, even from afar.

Tools that Enhance Remote Team Collaboration

The cornerstone of effective remote collaboration is the right set of tools. Explore various collaboration platforms that offer a range of functionalities, from real-time communication to project management. Tools like Slack for communication, Trello or Asana for task management, and Google Workspace for document collaboration can significantly enhance team coordination. The goal is to select tools that align with your team's workflow and communication style, enabling everyone to stay connected and informed.

Virtual Whiteboards and Brainstorming Platforms

Brainstorming and ideation are critical components of collaboration, and virtual whiteboards serve as the digital equivalent of a physical meeting room. Platforms like Miro or Jamboard allow team members to visually share and develop ideas in real-time, fostering creativity and innovation. These tools can be particularly effective for remote teams, providing a space for spontaneous collaboration and visual thinking.

Effective Use of Project Management Software

Project management software is the backbone of remote team collaboration, providing a centralized platform to track tasks, deadlines, and progress. Effective use of these tools requires more than just logging tasks; it involves setting clear objectives, assigning responsibilities, and monitoring progress in a transparent manner.

Training team members to utilize these tools effectively can lead to improved efficiency and accountability.

Ensuring Security and Privacy in Collaborative Tools

While collaboration tools are indispensable, they also pose potential risks to security and privacy. It's essential to choose tools that adhere to stringent security standards, protecting sensitive information from unauthorized access. Educate your team on best practices for security, such as using strong passwords, enabling two-factor authentication, and being vigilant about phishing attacks.

Case Studies of Successful Remote Collaboration Through Technology

To illustrate the transformative power of technology in enhancing remote collaboration, this section could include case studies from various industries. These real-life examples demonstrate how teams have leveraged collaborative tools to overcome challenges, improve productivity, and achieve their objectives, providing actionable insights and inspiration for readers to implement in their own remote work practices.

By integrating and optimizing these collaborative technologies, remote teams can achieve a level of synergy and efficiency that rivals, or even surpasses, traditional in-office collaboration. The key is to choose the right tools, ensure secure usage, and foster a culture of open communication and shared goals, enabling remote teams to thrive in a digital workspace.

Automating Routine Tasks

The automation of routine tasks can significantly enhance productivity and allow remote workers to focus on more strategic, high-value activities. This subchapter explores how remote professionals can identify automation opportunities and leverage technology to streamline their workflows, reduce manual effort, and minimize the likelihood of human error.

Introduction to Automation in a Remote Work Context

Automation in remote work involves using software tools to perform repetitive tasks without human intervention. This can range from organizing emails to scheduling social media posts or even managing data entry. Understanding the types of tasks that can be automated is the first step toward building a more efficient remote work environment.

Tools and Platforms for Automating Repetitive Tasks

Explore various automation tools that are suitable for remote work, such as Zapier, which connects different apps to automate workflows, or IFTTT, which creates conditional statements for automating tasks. Specific tools like Buffer for social media automation or HubSpot for marketing and sales activities can also be pivotal in reducing time spent on routine tasks.

Creating a Personal Automation Strategy

Developing a personal automation strategy involves identifying tasks that are repetitive and time-consuming, understanding the triggers for these tasks, and determining the desired outcomes. By mapping out these processes, you can create automated workflows that seamlessly integrate into your daily routine, freeing up time for more important work.

Measuring the Impact of Automation on Productivity

To truly understand the benefits of automation, it's crucial to measure its impact on your productivity. This can involve tracking the time saved by automating tasks, assessing the reduction in errors, or evaluating the increase in output. By quantifying the benefits, you can make informed decisions about further automation opportunities.

Ethical Considerations in Workplace Automation

While automation can bring significant benefits, it's important to consider its ethical implications, particularly in a remote work context. Issues such as job displacement, privacy concerns, and the potential for increased surveillance need to be addressed. Ensuring transparency about the use of automation tools and fostering open communication about their impact can help mitigate these concerns.

By embracing automation, remote workers can not only enhance their productivity but also improve the quality of their work life, focusing on tasks that require human insight and creativity. This subchapter provides a roadmap for identifying automation opportunities and implementing them effectively, ensuring that remote professionals can reap the full benefits of this technological advancement.

Future-Proofing Your Remote Work Setup

In the rapidly evolving world of remote work, future-proofing your setup is essential to remain adaptable and resilient in the face of technological changes. This subchapter provides strategies for anticipating future trends, creating a flexible remote work environment, and continuously adapting to new technologies to ensure sustained productivity and competitiveness in the digital workplace.

Anticipating Future Trends in Remote Work Technology

Staying informed about the latest trends in remote work technology is crucial for future-proofing your setup. Regularly researching and understanding emerging technologies in communication, collaboration, and productivity can provide insights into what the future work environment might look like. This knowledge helps in making informed decisions about which technologies to adopt and how to evolve your remote work practices.

Building a Flexible and Adaptable Work Environment

Creating a flexible remote work environment means setting up a workspace that can easily adapt to new technologies and work processes. This involves choosing software and tools that are scalable, interoperable, and easily upgradable. It also means cultivating a mindset of agility and openness to change, ensuring that you can quickly adapt to new working methods or tools as they become available.

The Role of Artificial Intelligence and Machine Learning

Understanding the potential impact of artificial intelligence (AI) and machine learning (ML) on remote work is essential for future-proofing your setup. These technologies are increasingly being used to automate complex tasks, provide insights from data, and enhance decision-making processes. Familiarizing yourself with AI and ML applications in your field can help you leverage these technologies to improve your productivity and efficiency.

Preparing for the Integration of VR and AR in Remote Work

Virtual reality (VR) and augmented reality (AR) are set to revolutionize remote work by offering immersive and interactive ways to collaborate and communicate. Preparing for their integration involves staying updated on the advancements in VR and AR technologies, understanding their potential applications in your industry, and being ready to adopt these technologies as they become more accessible and relevant to your work.

Staying Ahead of the Curve: A Guide to Continuous Technological Relevance

To ensure continuous technological relevance, commit to lifelong learning and regular upskilling. Participate in online courses, attend virtual conferences, and engage with professional communities to stay updated on technological advancements. Embrace a proactive approach to experimenting with new tools and methodologies, even if they are outside your comfort zone, to maintain a competitive edge in the remote work landscape.

By anticipating technological trends, building a flexible work environment, and continuously adapting to new technologies, you can future-proof your remote work setup, ensuring that you remain productive, efficient, and relevant in an ever-changing digital workplace.

Chapter 8: Fostering Innovation and Creativity in Remote Work

In the vast expanse of remote work, where the confines of traditional offices no longer bind us, lies a tremendous opportunity to redefine the landscape of innovation and creativity. "Fostering Innovation and Creativity in Remote Work" is a chapter dedicated to unraveling the strategies and practices that empower remote workers and teams to ignite their creative spark and foster a culture of innovation from afar.

The transition to remote work has not only altered our daily routines but also challenged us to rethink how we collaborate, create, and solve problems. In this new environment, where physical brainstorming sessions and spontaneous coffee break conversations are replaced by virtual meetings and digital chats, fostering a creative and innovative workspace demands deliberate effort and strategic thinking.

This chapter explores the foundational elements that constitute a fertile ground for innovation in a remote setting. It examines how the unique dynamics of remote work can be harnessed to encourage out-of-the-box thinking, facilitate groundbreaking collaborations, and drive forward-thinking solutions. From individual creativity exercises to collective ideation platforms, we'll delve into the tools and techniques that can transform your remote workspace into a hub of innovation.

We'll also tackle the challenges that come with fostering creativity in a digital realm, such as overcoming virtual communication barriers and ensuring that every team member feels heard and valued. By addressing these challenges head-on, we can unlock the full potential of our remote teams, enabling them to contribute bold ideas and innovative solutions that drive success.

Join us in this exploratory journey as we navigate the uncharted waters of remote work innovation. Whether you're a solo freelancer looking to inject creativity into your projects or part of a remote team striving for groundbreaking solutions, this chapter offers a wealth of insights and strategies to help you cultivate an environment where innovation thrives and creativity knows no bounds. Embrace the possibilities of remote work and transform your virtual workspace into a crucible of innovation and creative excellence.

Creating an Innovative Remote Work Culture

In a remote work environment, fostering a culture that champions innovation and creativity is both a challenge and an opportunity. This subchapter explores how remote workers and teams can cultivate an atmosphere that not only embraces but actively encourages innovative thinking and creative problem-solving, even when miles apart.

Principles of Innovation in a Remote Work Setting

Innovation in remote work begins with establishing core principles that define and guide the creative ethos of a team or individual. These principles should emphasize openness to new ideas, willingness to take calculated risks, and a commitment to continuous learning and improvement. By setting a clear expectation that innovation is valued and encouraged, you can create a foundation that nurtures creativity.

Building a Culture that Encourages Experimentation and Risk-Taking

A culture that fosters innovation is one that allows for experimentation and understands that not all ideas will lead to success. Encouraging team members to take risks and explore uncharted territories without fear of failure is crucial. This could involve setting aside dedicated time for brainstorming and experimentation, or establishing 'innovation labs' where team members can work on creative side projects.

Techniques for Fostering Creative Thinking Among Remote Teams

Creative thinking doesn't happen in a vacuum, especially in a remote setting. Employ techniques such as virtual brainstorming sessions, creative workshops, or innovation challenges to spark creativity. Utilize digital collaboration tools that allow team members to share and develop ideas asynchronously or in real-time, fostering a continuous flow of innovation.

Balancing Structure and Flexibility to Spur Innovation

While creativity often requires freedom and flexibility, some structure is necessary to turn innovative ideas into actionable outcomes. Establish processes that allow for flexibility in how work is done, while also providing a framework for evaluating and implementing innovative ideas. This balance ensures that creativity is not just encouraged but effectively channeled towards meaningful results.

Success Stories of Innovation in Remote-First Companies

Highlighting success stories within the company or in other remote-first organizations can serve as powerful motivation and provide valuable lessons on fostering innovation. Share case studies where remote teams have successfully innovated to solve problems or create new value, demonstrating the potential of remote work environments to be powerhouses of creativity and innovation.

By cultivating a remote work culture that values innovation and creativity, organizations can harness the collective intelligence and diverse perspectives of their teams, leading to groundbreaking solutions and a competitive edge in the ever-evolving business landscape.

Idea Generation and Collaborative Creativity

In the digital realm of remote work, generating ideas and fostering collaborative creativity requires intentional strategies and tools to simulate the dynamic synergy of in-person brainstorming. This subchapter delves into effective methods and platforms that facilitate idea generation and collective creativity among remote teams, ensuring that geographical distance does not hinder innovation.

Tools and Techniques for Remote Idea Generation

Leverage digital platforms specifically designed for brainstorming and idea generation. Tools like Mural or Miro offer virtual whiteboards where team members can contribute thoughts, sketch ideas, and build upon each other's concepts in real-time or asynchronously. Emphasize the use of diverse techniques such as mind mapping, SCAMPER, or the Six Thinking Hats to stimulate creative thinking and generate a breadth of ideas.

Organizing Virtual Brainstorming Sessions and Innovation Workshops

Plan and execute virtual brainstorming sessions that mimic the energy and interaction of in-person workshops. Establish clear objectives for each session and use breakout rooms to facilitate smaller group discussions. Employ virtual facilitators to guide the sessions, ensuring that every voice is heard and ideas are captured efficiently. Incorporate interactive elements such as polls, quizzes, or gamified challenges to maintain engagement and stimulate creativity.

Encouraging Diverse Perspectives for Richer Ideation

Diversity is a key driver of innovation. Create an environment where team members from different backgrounds, departments, or areas of expertise can contribute ideas. Encourage cross-pollination of thoughts by hosting cross-functional brainstorming sessions, allowing team members to bring unique perspectives and challenge conventional thinking, leading to more comprehensive and innovative solutions.

Documenting and Managing Ideas in a Remote Environment

Efficiently managing and documenting ideas is crucial in a remote setting. Utilize digital tools to capture and organize ideas generated during brainstorming sessions. Ensure there is a clear process for evaluating, selecting, and progressing ideas to the next stages of development. Regularly review the idea repository to identify patterns, themes, or opportunities that might have been overlooked.

From Idea to Action: Prioritizing and Implementing Creative Solutions

Transitioning from idea generation to implementation is a critical step in the innovation process. Establish criteria for evaluating ideas based on their feasibility, impact, and alignment with organizational goals. Prioritize ideas that promise the most value and outline clear action plans for their execution. Foster a sense of ownership by involving team members who contributed ideas in the implementation process, ensuring they have the resources and support needed to bring their concepts to fruition.

By adopting these strategies and tools, remote teams can overcome the barriers of distance and cultivate a vibrant culture of collaborative creativity, turning a collection of individual contributors into a cohesive, innovative force.

Design Thinking in Remote Work

Design thinking offers a solution-oriented approach that can be particularly effective in remote work environments, where traditional methods of collaboration are transformed into virtual interactions. This subchapter explores how remote teams can apply design thinking principles to foster innovation and solve complex challenges creatively and empathetically.

Adapting Design Thinking Principles to Remote Settings

Introduce the five stages of design thinking—Empathize, Define, Ideate, Prototype, and Test—to your remote team, and adapt these stages for virtual collaboration. Emphasize the importance of empathy in understanding user needs and challenges and leverage digital tools to gather insights and share findings. For instance, virtual interviews or surveys can help teams empathize with users' perspectives, even from a distance.

Running Virtual Design Sprints

Design sprints can be a powerful way to accelerate problem-solving and innovation in remote teams. Guide teams on how to conduct virtual design sprints, including setting clear goals, scheduling structured activities, and using online collaboration platforms for sprint exercises. Encourage the use of virtual prototypes, which can be rapidly developed and tested with users in a remote context.

User-centric Innovation from Afar

Maintain a user-centric focus by involving users in the remote innovation process. Utilize digital tools to engage users in ideation sessions or to gather feedback on prototypes. This can include virtual user testing, online feedback forms, or interactive webinars where users can share their experiences and insights, ensuring that the solutions developed are deeply aligned with their needs.

Case Studies of Remote Design Thinking Success

Highlight examples of remote teams successfully employing design thinking to solve problems and innovate. These case studies can illustrate best practices, common challenges, and the tangible impacts of using design thinking in a remote context. Sharing these stories can inspire teams and provide practical insights into how design thinking can be effectively applied remotely.

Overcoming Challenges in Remote Design Thinking Processes

Address common obstacles that remote teams may face when implementing design thinking, such as fostering empathy from a distance or collaborating effectively during ideation and prototyping stages. Offer strategies to overcome these challenges, such as using rich media to convey user stories, employing synchronous and asynchronous collaboration tools, and establishing clear communication and feedback loops to keep team members aligned and engaged throughout the design thinking process.

By integrating design thinking into their remote work practices, teams can harness a powerful framework for innovation that is collaborative, user-centered, and adaptable to the unique dynamics of virtual teamwork. This approach not only fosters creative problem-solving but also strengthens team cohesion and ensures that solutions are deeply attuned to user needs and contexts.

Leveraging Cross-Industry Insights

Innovation often stems from the intersection of diverse fields and industries. For remote teams, the virtual environment offers a unique opportunity to tap into a vast array of cross-industry insights, which can ignite creative problem-solving and introduce novel approaches to challenges. This subchapter explores how remote workers can leverage insights from various sectors to foster a culture of innovation and creativity.

Learning from Other Industries to Enhance Creative Problem-Solving

Encourage remote teams to look beyond their industry's boundaries for inspiration and innovative practices. Highlight how solutions in one field can be adapted to address challenges in another. For example, the agile methodologies used in software development can inspire project management approaches in marketing teams, or user experience design principles in tech can enhance customer service strategies in the retail sector.

Strategies for Cross-Industry Collaboration in a Remote Context

Facilitate cross-industry collaboration by setting up virtual think tanks or joint workshops with professionals from different sectors. Use online platforms to host cross-industry innovation sessions, where participants can share challenges, insights, and best practices from their fields, fostering a fertile ground for cross-pollination of ideas.

Case Studies of Cross-Industry Innovation Benefiting Remote Work

Present case studies that showcase successful cross-industry innovations, particularly those that have enhanced remote work practices. These examples can serve as powerful illustrations of how integrating disparate insights can lead to breakthrough solutions, encouraging teams to think more broadly and creatively in their problem-solving efforts.

Building a Personal Network for Cross-Industry Insights

Guide remote professionals on how to build and engage with a diverse professional network that spans various industries. Encourage participation in online forums, webinars, and virtual conferences that draw a cross-industry audience. Emphasize the value of actively listening and engaging with professionals from different sectors to gather a broad range of insights and perspectives.

Organizing Virtual Cross-Industry Exchange Programs

Propose the organization of virtual exchange programs, where team members can temporarily immerse themselves in a different industry environment, such as through virtual job shadowing or collaboration on a project. These experiences can provide deep insights into different industry practices and challenges, sparking innovative ideas and approaches that can be applied in their primary field of work.

By actively engaging with and learning from other industries, remote teams can break free from the echo chamber of their own sector, uncovering fresh perspectives and innovative solutions that can be applied to their work, driving creativity, and fostering a culture of continuous learning and innovation.

Measuring and Encouraging Innovation

While fostering a culture of innovation and creativity is vital in a remote work environment, equally important is establishing a framework to measure and nurture this innovative spirit. This subchapter outlines methods to assess the impact of innovation within remote teams and strategies to continuously encourage and reward creative problem-solving and innovative thinking.

Metrics and KPIs for Tracking Innovation in Remote Settings

Developing key performance indicators (KPIs) specific to innovation can help remote teams quantify their progress. These metrics might include the number of new ideas generated, the percentage of ideas moved to experimentation, or the impact of implemented innovations on efficiency and outcomes. Establishing clear metrics provides a tangible way to assess the effectiveness of your team's creative efforts.

Recognizing and Rewarding Creativity and Innovation in Remote Teams

Recognition plays a crucial role in reinforcing innovative behavior. Implement a system to celebrate and reward team members who contribute novel ideas or drive successful innovations. This could range from public acknowledgments in virtual meetings to tangible rewards for ideas that yield significant improvements or results, fostering a culture where innovation is not just encouraged but celebrated.

Feedback Mechanisms to Encourage Continuous Improvement

Constructive feedback is essential for refining ideas and fostering a culture of continuous innovation. Establish regular review sessions where team members can present their ideas and receive input from peers. Encourage a positive feedback loop where constructive criticism is welcomed and seen as a steppingstone for further innovation.

Balancing Innovation with Day-to-Day Operations

While innovation is critical, it's essential to balance it with the day-to-day operational needs of the team. Help teams allocate time effectively between routine tasks and innovative projects. This balance ensures that while creativity is nurtured, the core functions and responsibilities of the team are not compromised.

Creating a Sustainable Model for Remote Work Innovation

For innovation to be sustainable, it needs to be ingrained in the team's ethos and workflow. Encourage an environment where team members feel empowered to experiment and where failure is seen as a learning opportunity. Embedding innovation into the team's DNA requires continuous encouragement, the right resources, and a supportive leadership approach that champions creative thinking and problem-solving.

By measuring and encouraging innovation actively, remote teams can not only track their progress but also create an environment where creativity is a fundamental aspect of their work culture. This not only drives growth and success but also enhances job satisfaction and engagement among team members, making the remote work experience more fulfilling and productive.

Conclusion

Congratulations on reaching this point! We've explored extensive aspects of enhancing your remote work experience. Wondering where to begin? Here are five effective starting points to create a more satisfying and productive remote work environment:

1. **Prioritize Daily Goals**: Start each day by identifying the three most critical tasks you aim to accomplish. If multiple tasks vie for your attention, select one that aligns closely with a significant professional objective. Dedicate your most productive hour—the time when you're most energized and focused—to this task, leveraging the opportunity to demonstrate your capabilities to supervisors or clients.

2. **Evaluate Your Meetings**: Reassess your upcoming video calls for the next week. Determine if any meetings could be streamlined or if your presence is essential. Discuss with your supervisor alternative approaches, such as providing vital information beforehand or receiving a summary of action items post-meeting. If reducing meeting frequency isn't feasible, prepare by noting your intended

contributions or objectives for each meeting to enhance focus and productivity.

3. **Streamline Your Inbox**: Dedicate just five minutes to set up an email filtering rule to reduce clutter. For instance, automatically direct emails containing "unsubscribe" to a designated "Newsletters" folder. Gradually implement similar rules to ensure your inbox contains only immediately relevant emails.

4. **Change Your Environment**: If you're in the habit of working from the same spot daily, consider altering your surroundings. This could mean working from a café, a friend's place, or simply a different area in your home. Even minor changes, like relocating to another side of your table or refreshing your workspace with a personal item, followed by a brief walk, can rejuvenate your work environment.

5. **Incorporate Personal Happiness**: Actively choose an activity that boosts your personal joy and energy while working remotely. This might be scheduling daily walks, arranging co-working sessions with a friend, or preparing enjoyable and nutritious meals in advance to enhance your afternoon productivity.

These approaches are not just about improving your work output but also about nurturing a more balanced and fulfilling remote work lifestyle.

Aim to adopt a new habit weekly to enhance your remote work experience continually. By doing so, you're not only refining your personal work routine but also contributing to a more positive and healthy organizational culture. Moreover, you're participating in shaping a global perspective that recognizes and supports the need for every individual to develop their distinct, sustainable, and efficient work-life strategy.

www.ingramcontent.com/pod-product-compliance
Lightning Source LLC
Chambersburg PA
CBHW050324230526
45471CB00005B/2332